WE

CAN

TALK

Tips for enhancing your child's speech
and language
Rachel Arntson, M.S., CCC-SLP

ISBN 10: 0-9825071-9-4
ISBN 13: 978-0-9825071-9-3

Printed in the United States of America

Published by Talk It Rock It, LLC

P.O. Box 1734, Maple Grove, MN USA

www.TalkItRockIt.com

I dedicate this book to my children, Jacob, Kelsey, and Erik, who taught me about speech and language in a playful way, and to my husband, Doug, who is my support and my calm.

"May your conversations be rich and may your joy overflow as you watch your children learn and grow."

Rachel Arntson

Thank You

There are so many people throughout the years who have contributed to the information in this book. Literally thousands of people including teachers, professors, speech-language pathologists, friends, family, and children, all have their imprint on these pages. For their wisdom and support, I am eternally grateful. I thank my dear friends in Early Childhood Special Education for being the best teammates anyone could ever have. Thank you to Trish Hargrove, Bonnie Lund, Jada Jokumsen-Steinle, and Rebecca Simmons from Minnesota State University – Mankato for supporting me, offering advice, and for studying my ideas. I especially thank the parents of the young children with whom I have worked over the years for sharing their biggest gifts with me – their children.

I also thank Amy Pederson for her ability to provide insight through the eyes of a parent and professional, and Jacob Arntson for getting this book ready to print. Thank you to Betty Liedtke for her extraordinary talent of proofing, correcting, and re-wording.

Introduction

All children, regardless of their ability or inability to talk, communicate in some way. When children cry, throw tantrums, give you a toy, or walk away, they are all communicating something. Our challenge is to observe our children, look at all their responses and reactions to the world, and then determine how to help them reach the next level of communication.

Parents, you know your child better than anyone. You can see by the look on his face or by his body language whether he is happy or uncomfortable with something. Because you know your child so well, it is humbling to write a book telling parents how to communicate more effectively with their children. Parents start with knowledge about their child far beyond what any speech-language pathologist can know. So it is with humility that I present to you **WE CAN TALK** – Tips for Enhancing Your Child's Speech and Language.

WE CAN TALK became a reality because of almost 30 years of working with young children and their families. Parents have taught me much over the years, and I have been honored to be the recipient of their wisdom. This book is an attempt to share what I discuss with parents and what we as a team do to help children during speech-language therapy home visits. Below is a thank you letter I received this past year from a parent of one of my students. It expresses perfectly the goal we all have for all of our children – to be the best communicators they can be and to create an interaction with the people who love them.

Dear Rachel,

You taught me so many amazing skills, and they have definitely had a wonderful impact on my child's life. I feel like I understand how to get the most out of the interactions I have with her. Like most parents I want to feel connected to my child, and there is no doubt I learned the means to make this possible while I was working with you. I describe it to others by telling them it is like I had a child born to me that spoke another language, and you were the person who taught me how to speak her language. The word "coach" seems so perfect!

It would be like me trying to save my child from drowning without knowing how to swim myself. You were my life vest. You taught me how to get through this and how to see the bright side. You reminded me that there is so much hope for my little girl. When we met you, I felt like I was sinking fast in a sea of information. But throughout our year together, I learned the necessary things to get my child and me both out of the water safely! I am now confident in my ability to be the best mommy I can be for my daughter.

I will simply say "thank you" for teaching me how to communicate with her. Thank you for showing me so many fun things to do with her to get her to connect with me. Thank you for helping me feel confident about the care I give her, and thank you for always taking the extra time we needed and wanted from you during our sessions. We will never forget the difference you made in our family!

Sincerely,
Heidi Segedy

Letters like this prompted me to finally write down all of the techniques that I have learned over the years. I placed these techniques into a format that parents of children with speech and language delays can easily understand and implement. What has resulted is a guidebook for all parents, whether your child has speech and language delays or not.

My goal was to also provide a format that other professionals, including speech-language pathologists and early childhood teachers, could share with their students and families. WE CAN TALK is very simply my "tricks of the trade" that I have learned and feel compelled to offer others.

When applying the WE CAN TALK techniques, you can become a better listener and observer of your child's life and her desires. You will also be able to identify what helps your child become verbal and what hinders her. You will essentially become your child's Sherlock Holmes, uncovering the mystery of how to help your child learn to communicate.

In this manual you will learn 9 strategies and techniques that will guide you along the road to helping your child learn to communicate. Focus on one technique per week – experiment with it in virtually every part of your child's day. Use it while getting your child dressed, while having a meal, during bath time, while playing, when traveling in the car, when going for walks, anytime! Concentrate on only one technique at a time, and you will be amazed at what you will learn about your child's speech and language skills. WE CAN TALK techniques are practical and simple to learn, but they do require one thing to make them a habit – practice. These techniques do not require any more time OUT of your day, but they do require incorporating them INTO your day. Enjoy!

"The best way to change our child's communication ability or behavior is to first change our own."
Rachel Arntson

What others have said about the WE CAN TALK techniques, presentations, and other Talk It Rock It products:

WE CAN TALK is an excellent resource for parents and professionals seeking to enhance speech and language development in children! Congratulations, Rachel, on another high quality product.
Bonnie Lund, PhD, CCC-SLP, Associate Professor, MSU, Mankato

She's done it again! Rachel Arntson is among the most gifted clinicians I've had the pleasure of working with in my thirty years as a speech-language pathologist. In WE CAN TALK, she has masterfully analyzed this thing we call speech therapy. She has figured out how to describe the intuition, turn-taking and reinforcement that goes into therapy, in easy-to-follow steps, so that parents may experience the ultimate joy of teaching their child to communicate. WE CAN TALK is a must-have tool kit for any parent or professional interested in getting kids talking!
Susan Field, MS, CCC-SLP, East Lansing, Michigan

What I like best about the WE CAN TALK program is the simplicity. Rachel provides a detailed step-by-step outline of techniques that a beginning speech-language clinician such as myself can clearly understand and use successfully without feeling overwhelmed.
Jada Jokumsen-Steinle, M.S.,
Clinical Fellow-Speech-Language Pathologist

WE CAN TALK not only provides great techniques for parents, but also for student clinicians in the field of speech-language pathology and special education. WE CAN TALK techniques are easy to implement into therapy sessions.
Rebecca Simmons, M.S., Clinical Fellow-Speech-Language Pathologist

I want to commend Rachel Arntson on a FABULOUS presentation. It was practical, energetic, fun, and down-to-earth. I can't tell you how much I loved it. I can tell that Rachel is continually working on new therapy methods! If only more people in our profession were as willing to expose themselves and teach actual intervention with real, live examples.
Susan Thomsen, Speech-Language Pathologist, California

We had a fabulous time hosting the conference presented by Rachel Arntson. Personable, informative, down-to-earth, and entertaining are just a few words that come to mind when I think of Rachel. The feedback that we received from the participants that attended this course reminded us why we host conferences. Never have we had so many participants come up to us with big smiles reporting that "this was the best conference I have ever attended," or "Thank you for finding her." So a big thank you, thank you, thank you.
Organizer of a conference held on Long Island, New York

Your products are fantastic. They are perfectly designed to encourage speech and language development from a basic level on up.
Ellen Langendorfer, Speech-Language Pathologist

I have worked as a Speech Pathologist for nearly thirty years. Talk It Rock It products have helped me teach students with autism how to communicate more than any product or approach I have ever used. Thanks for giving children the opportunity to experience the 'power of communication.'

Cynthia A. Owens, Speech-Language Pathologist, Fairview, West Virginia

Contents

WE CAN TALK

Chapter 1

Wait, Watch, and Wonder about what your child is communicating.

This technique is perhaps the hardest because at this point, all it requires is to simply **watch** your child and analyze what he is doing to communicate. It is so difficult to just stand there and watch and not anticipate your child's needs when you already know what he wants. But once in a while, it is important to simply observe what your child does when you wait for him to tell or show you his needs. It is important to look at just how much he is attempting to interact with others, how often he is responding to others, and how much he is just roaming independently and avoiding interactions with others. The best way to do that is to **wonder** by **waiting** and **watching**. Let's get started with Step 1.

W - WAIT, WATCH, and WONDER.

Several times in a day, take some time to just **wait** and **watch** your child as he "does his thing." What exactly is he doing? Think of his actions as well as any verbalizing you hear. Take some time to WONDER about what you think he may be communicating. Write down some of the frequent ways your child lets you know what he wants during his day. What does he do? What does he say?

_____

_____

_____

_____

Now **wonder** about what your child would do if you made no requirements of him. If your child were able to choose anything to do all day, what would he choose to do? Write down several things that you know he loves.

_____

_____

_____

_____

_____

HOW do you know that he loves those activities or things? How does he show you that he loves them? And how does he show you what he dislikes? Write them down.

_____

_____

_____

_____

_____

WAIT – Now choose a specific activity to do with your child (choose something from your list above of things he loves). Whether you are playing with a toy, having a snack, walking to the park, or doing something else, occasionally stop in the middle of the activity and **wait**. Don't do a thing. Just **wait**. Do not anticipate your child's desires. **Waiting** is an important strategy to enhance your child's verbal and non-verbal communication skills.

Examples:

• During snack time, give your child a few pieces of the snack and then wait to see what he does.

• While your child is swinging, stop swinging him and wait to see what he does.

WATCH – Now it's time to **watch**. Which of these behaviors does your child show during activities he loves and during other daily routines when you **wait** in the middle of the activity? What do you see and hear? Does he....

- ❑ Walk away
- ❑ Scream or cry
- ❑ Smile or laugh
- ❑ Look at you
- ❑ Reach for the object with his hands
- ❑ Pull you to what he wants
- ❑ Point to the object he wants
- ❑ Move his body
- ❑ Verbalize

Which of these behaviors do you see the most?

_____

_____

Which behaviors would you prefer to see more often?

_____

_____

WONDER – Now let's **wonder** about what your child is communicating, whether others would understand what he is telling you, and how you can help him get to the next level of communicating and interacting with others. **Wondering** involves brainstorming about the possibilities and experimenting – figuring out what works and what doesn't work. Sometimes we arrive at incredible solutions. The specifics of how to get him to the next level of communicating will be described in many of the other techniques in WE CAN TALK, but here are some examples of how to brainstorm and **wonder** what your child is communicating and how to get him to the next level.

Examples:

- If your child walks away, he is possibly telling you that: 1) This activity is not exciting enough to stay. 2) This activity makes him too uncomfortable to stay. 3) Interacting with people for too long makes him uncomfortable. 4) He doesn't know what else to do to let you know he enjoyed it. To increase his "staying power," you may want to try singing a song paired with that activity, use varied inflection and excitement in your voice and gestures, or try a different activity to keep him engaged.

- If your child screams, he may be telling you that he is angry that you stopped and that he wants you to keep going with the activity. You will want to help him tell you he wants more by possibly teaching him a strategy of "giving you 5" to start the activity again. Or you may want to teach him a sign to indicate that he wants more. Finally, you could also say a word, making sure that your child is watching you and listening to the word you say.

- If your child moves his body but doesn't verbalize to get something, he is telling you clearly that he wants to do the activity but cannot combine that gesture with a sound. You will want to pair that movement with a word, phrase, sound, or song that he can start to imitate. The word or sound you say should be enticing and full of energy so that your child pays attention to it. You can also ask your child to say the word or phrase you are modeling for him.

Be positive and be careful
of withholding or forcing.

There is a very fine line you will walk between withholding things from children – forcing them to say or do something before you give it to them – and, in contrast, enticing them to attempt a different form of communication or teaching them the skills to improve their level of interaction. If you choose a style of withholding things in a punitive way until they do what you say, this is a battle that you are sure to lose. It creates a negative form of interaction that you do not want to reinforce. You should, though, try to get your child to say a word. Just remember that if your child refuses to attempt it, you are possibly asking too much too soon. Start with baby steps. You may want to request something a bit easier like a "give me 5," as listed above, and then praise him for his attempt. This will help your child learn that complying to your requests will pay off. When your child learns this, then you can begin to practice requesting the verbal attempts.

Teachable and un-teachable moments.

An important concept to consider is the phrase "teachable moment." A teachable moment occurs when you have figured out what your child wants. An "un-teachable moment" occurs when your child obviously wants something, and you simply cannot determine what it is. Un-teachable moments can be very frustrating for both you and your child. Those are the times when you may need to change the subject, try to distract your child to get him interested in something else, apologize for not understanding, or see if he can show you what he wants.

In contrast, a teachable moment is a true gift because your child has actually succeeded in letting you know what he needs. You then have two choices: 1) Immediately give your child whatever it is that he wants. 2) Help your child communicate his need at a higher level than how he is currently communicating. In any given situation, you will likely alternate between these two choices. Take advantage whenever you can, though, to choose the second option and teach your child through the teachable moments. The more he learns through the teachable moments, the less frequently you will see the un-teachable moments.

Let's illustrate a teachable moment with a specific example. If your child leads you to the back door, he is probably letting you know he wants to go outside. That is a teachable moment. What can you do to help him communicate this desire at a higher level? There are many possibilities. You could ask him a question such as, "Do you want to go outside?" If he smiles at you, giving you the indication that you guessed correctly, then you could show him how to knock on the door to request that you open it. Show him how to knock by combining the gesture of knocking with the words, "knock knock." You could say a word such as "open", use a gesture with the word, and then wait for a few seconds to see what your child does. You could also ask him to imitate a word such as "outside" or "open." A child can get frustrated though, if they don't know how to imitate. You want to keep your child as calm as possible as you teach him, so asking him to imitate may be too difficult. Perhaps have him follow a verbal direction by saying, "If you want to go outside, then go get your shoes." Model whatever your child will have success doing and praise him for his attempts.

The possibilities of what you can do are endless, and we will describe more of these with the additional techniques coming later in this book. But first, just **wonder** about what he is communicating by **waiting** and **watching** him. That is the first and most important step to learn right now. Now that you know HOW your child communicates and WHAT he is communicating, the remaining techniques will teach you what to do next. In conclusion, teach yourself to SLOW DOWN so you can **wonder**, **wait**, and **watch** closely the communication you see in your child.

WE CAN TALK

Chapter 2

Examine your position. Exaggerate and entice with your gestures and voice.

Some children do not show awareness when people talk to them. Others do not watch, stay engaged, or show an interest in what others are doing. There are also other children who ARE observant of people but are limited in their expressive vocabulary, have difficulty pronouncing words, or are unable to imitate what others do or say. Regardless of your child's ability to watch and copy people, she can benefit from this technique. In order to learn and communicate effectively with others, children need to pay attention to your face, your actions, the different sounds you make, and your words. That state of "watchfulness" sets the stage for imitation.

How do you help your child be "watchful" and notice the things that you say and do? Examine your position.

The easy answer is this: you need to be more interesting than all of the other distractions in your child's world. It's easy to say but not as easy to put into practice. You should think about how you can make your voice and gestures more exciting, but first look at how you are positioned.

When talking to your child, give him every advantage to be attentive to what you are saying. You can do that by positioning yourself at your child's level. When he tries to get your attention, lower your body to show your child that you are interested in what he has to say. When you are giving him a verbal direction, maximize his attention by first positioning yourself in front of your child before you begin talking. He may need you to tap him on the shoulder or hold his hands before giving the direction.

When looking at books with your child, positioning may be something to consider. Some children have difficulty shifting their eye gaze from objects to people. When an object is in front of a child such as a book, he may become so involved with the book that he is not interacting or aware of others looking at the book with him. If that is an issue with your child, consider sitting across from him as opposed to having him sit on your lap. When playing with your child, also sit in front of him, so he can more easily look up at your when you talk to him. Position is important in every activity you do.

What gets your child's attention or interest?

Think about activities you have done with your child or things you have said that have attracted her attention or that make her copy you. (Especially note those times when she looks, smiles, laughs at you, does what you do, or imitates your words. Also refer to the activities you noted in the first technique – **Wonder about what your child is communicating. Wait and Watch**.) List those activities.

_____

_____

_____

_____

In the activities listed above, why do you think your child pays attention or copies you during those times? What are the strategies that seem to work? Is it the words you say, how you say them, or how you use gestures?

_____

_____

_____

_____

Now think about how you might try those same strategies in other activities or daily routines. Much of what you do may fit the technique of exaggerating and enticing with your gestures and voice. Write down some ideas.

_____

_____

_____

_____

Are there any objects that your child especially enjoys and can play with for long periods of time? List them.

_____

_____

_____

_____

If there are objects that your child really enjoys, how might you be able to participate with your child using those objects? Think about ways to **exaggerate** and **entice** with your voice and gestures using those objects. Think about your position as well.

Using activities your child loves will be excellent motivators for increasing your child's desire to stay with an activity and notice you. The goals of this second technique are to:

1. Increase your child's ability to watch and listen to others.

2. Increase your child's ability to imitate and spontaneously use gestures and verbalizations.
3. Increase the number of activities and the amount of time that a child can stay with an activity, especially activities involving you.

You often have to trick children into imitating you by getting them so enthralled with what you are doing that they can't stand NOT to attempt it themselves. There are two things to think about to achieve the three goals listed above: **Exaggerate** your **gestures** and **exaggerate** your **voice**. Let's discuss some of the different ways you can exaggerate with your gestures and voice to entice your child to imitate.

Exaggerate your gestures.

Think about the types of exaggerated movements you can make during play and during daily routines to get your child to watch what you are doing and imitate. Also, when choosing toys and activities, keep in mind that those with multiple pieces or those that can be repeated multiple times are excellent. Repetition is often needed to encourage imitation skills.

- During a daily routine like bath time, think about how you can make any bath toys (ducks or fish) swim, walk, jump, or fly, and exaggerate the motion to attract your child's attention.

- In anything you do, talk with your hands and your facial expressions. Be as animated as you can. Your comfort level with this kind of silliness will dictate how much you use gestures. Your child's reaction will dictate how much or how little exaggeration is needed to attract his attention.

- Try a "clean up" game by putting objects such as blocks in a container. First think about how many different ways you can put a block in a box. Be creative by making the objects fly, jump, move like a car, etc. (Remember to use activities or toys that are motivating to your child – blocks may not be the best toy for your child. Use your list above of enjoyable activities or objects.)

- Another possible activity would be to put something silly on your head and "sneeze" it off while saying "ahchoo." Did your child notice you? Did she laugh? Did she indicate that she wanted you to do it again? If she is motivated to watch you, give the object to her to see if she'll try to copy you.

- To keep your child with you, do something different with the object she is interested in. Perhaps hide the object in her shirt to keep her searching for it.

- Other large motor activities such as playing chase games, swinging your child, flying like an airplane, or moving like animals on the ground are wonderful activities to help your child notice you. Also try imitating your child's motor movements at times, as this may be the best way to start imitation.

- You can also exaggerate your gestures by holding objects up to your face, naming the objects before giving them to your child. You could also give the object to your child first, and as she is holding the object, hold her hand and the object to your face while you say the word. The cue of seeing your face may be what she needs to really listen to the word and visualize how it is pronounced. After doing that, you can try taking her hand and the object up to her face and telling her, "Your turn," to see if she will try to copy you.

- Teaching your child sign language is an excellent way to encourage imitation, and studies show that signing does not interfere with speech and language development. In fact, it enhances it.

- Another key factor in helping your child be more watchful of others is to teach her to pay attention to **pointing**. While holding your child, point to objects by doing "tours of the house," watching if your child is able to follow your pointing. When you are outside and hear different noises such as cars or airplanes, point to them. When you see interesting objects, point to them. Also, when you are performing daily routines around the house, teach your child to put things in particular places by pointing and saying, "Put it right here." When showing your child a book, increase her ability to follow a point: **Exaggerate your pointing** by tickling the pictures, patting them, and knocking on them. How many different ways can you **exaggerate** how you point to things? Try several ways and watch your child's reaction.

- Teach your child to give her hand to you when you are giving her an object/item that she wants. Asking for her hand increases a child's ability to watch you and gives her a cue that there is a connection between a person and the object that she desires. The physical connection of holding her hand while giving her things such as snacks or toys gives your child the awareness that YOU are the one giving it to her. As simple as that sounds, this ability to shift between desired objects and people is harder to learn in some situations than one might think. As you give your child snacks or objects, name them, use sound effects, and exaggerate your movements as you try to maintain her attention.

Pair your gestures with sounds or words.

At first, children may have an easier time imitating gestures than sounds or words. If you pair the gestures with an enticing sound or word, it will increase the likelihood that your child will attempt to imitate the sound as well as the gesture. All of the activities listed above should be accompanied often by a sound, word, or phrase. Gestures are important to include because you can usually physically help your child imitate a gesture. When your child refuses or does not respond to gestural or verbal imitation, you can say, "I will help you do it," and grab her hand to do the imitation of the motor movement. Verbal imitation does not have that advantage.

Exaggerate, entertain, and entice with your voice.

When you talk to your child, think about how you speak and how exciting your voice sounds. When you exaggerate or entice with your voice, though, don't distort your voice or words to the point that your child doesn't understand you. Distortion is NOT what we are recommending. We are recommending a bit more animation and excitement to your voice and words. Sometimes an "exaggeration" may involve whispering, speaking more slowly, and using more inflection in the words you say. Be animated!

• Put added emphasis on sounds in a word, making the word sound like its meaning. For example, when saying the word "pop" during bubble blowing, produce it like the sound of a bubble popping. Make the word "come to life."

• You can also extend vowels or consonants (like "m," "n," and "s") in words to give added emphasis to those sounds. For example, if I were saying the word "milk" during meal time, I might emphasize the "m" in the word by saying "mmmmmilk," rubbing my tummy while I said the word to give the visual effect of indicating that the milk is "yummy". This technique is especially good with children who are having difficulty producing a particular word or a particular sound in a word.

- How you model or exaggerate a word depends on how your child currently produces it. For example, if your child says "at" for "hat," you may want to exaggerate the "h" sound by blowing the air on your hand while you say the word. If your child says "ha" for "hat," then you will want to exaggerate the final "t" sound by tapping your mouth or your child's leg while saying "t" and saying it more loudly.

- Invite your child to copy you at times. It's OK to say, "Your turn" or "Do it with me," to let your child know that you are confident he can try. Positive encouragement is different, though, than pressure to imitate. And remember that gestures are great because you can physically help children imitate gestures.

- Exaggerating your voice can be done naturally with music and while reading to your child. This will be discussed more completely with the techniques dedicated to books and music. However, begin to think about using music and books to help your child be more watchful and imitate.

- Whispering your words can sometimes be enticing for children to attempt to imitate.

- Slow down. Children need speech presented more slowly in order for them to imitate.

List some times during the day and some of the words and gestures that you will be exaggerating throughout this week. Perhaps focus on words and activities that your child found the most motivating. Pick an activity, such as going to the grocery store or playing with Play Doh, and write down some of the ways you can say certain sounds, words, or phrases related to those activities. For example, try several ways to say "apple."

_____

_____

_____

Is your child showing good BALANCE?

In this technique you want to help your child learn to watch your gestures and listen to the words and sounds you and others say. Sometimes children show ability to hyper-focus on toys or certain objects but are very limited in the ability to focus on you or other people. The important thing to look for in all areas of communication is BALANCE! A child who can stay attentive to a specific activity for long periods of time can have a wonderful gift of great concentration or an interference in her ability to learn because she cannot focus on people. Ask yourself these questions:

1. Does my child focus on some activities SO MUCH that it does not allow her to explore other toys or other uses of toys?

2. Does my child focus so much on certain toys or objects that it is difficult to get her to watch me?

If your answer is yes, then your goal will be two-fold: 1) Expand her ability to be watchful of a wide variety of toys and activities. 2) Expand her ability to shift her attention from her desired objects to people. Your goal will be to make WHAT you do with the object more fun than the object itself.

Building on Techniques 1 and 2. As you **examine** your position and **exaggerate** and **entice** with your voice and gestures, also combine that with Technique 1 by **waiting** and **watching** to see if your child responds with imitation or any other response. Remember that even a smile is a response, and that tells you your child is engaged and enjoying the interaction you created with her. Occasionally say "Your turn" or "You do it" to your child. Give her that look of eager anticipation as you wait to see what kind of turn she will take.

You have now completed the first two techniques. Try to combine both of them during your daily routines and move on to Technique Number 3.

Chapter 3

Comment about what you and your child are doing, seeing, and enjoying.

"Commenting" is for all children, from the very verbal ones to the silent observers. There are some children who just won't imitate or attempt to say words for whatever reason. Parents may have tried all of the exaggeration and enticement with their gestures and voice, and their child is still not responding vocally. There are other children who are beginning to respond to their parents' exaggeration and enticement techniques but are imitating and attempting to say words inconsistently. Whether your child is quiet, occasionally imitating, or very verbal, you may want to change your focus and put your energy into this technique. Concentrate on one thing – putting words and knowledge into your child's head. Don't worry about the imitation or the responding right now. Just give your child vocabulary and descriptions of what he is doing, seeing, and enjoying.

Research has found that adults tend to speak less often and also more simply to children who have limited verbal skills. Because these "quiet" children don't respond in the same way that other children do, our tendency is also to speak less. It's difficult to have a conversation with yourself, so as a result we, too, become quiet. But children need to hear words and descriptions about their world, even if they cannot say the words themselves. A phenomenal study by Hart and Risley (1999, *The Social World of Children Learning to Talk*) showed that children from language-rich environments heard 2,100 words per hour, whereas the contrast of 600 words per hour occurred in homes that were not rich in word use. (Language-rich environments exclude words that may be heard on TV but instead relate only to words used in direct interaction with people.) These results also directly correlated with children who became stronger readers.

Children need to know the richness of words. As parents, we need to consciously choose what we are going to do in terms of talking to our children. In addition, we need to make decisions about how much TV watching is acceptable in our homes. We need to believe wholeheartedly that the time we take for our children at a young age will have a direct effect on our children's success later in school and in life. All children, regardless of verbal ability, need to be enriched with this technique.

Why is commenting so important? Children need to understand the words we say in order for them to finally say the words. Remember that those children who have an understanding of literally thousands of words are also the children who are more equipped to become strong readers.

Talk about the objects in your child's world.

Take your child's lead and begin talking about the things your child loves and is doing. When your child is playing with a toy or participating in a daily routine like getting dressed, eating, or taking a bath, name all of the objects. Vary how you name an object. For example, a car can also be a vehicle or an automobile. Also begin naming the parts to the objects. You can point out the doors, wipers, lights, wheels, and trunk of the car. The object names you can use are endless. Also, talk about what the objects are made of, where they come from, and how they are used.

Repeat, repeat, repeat.

Think about what words would be important for your child to understand and learn to say. Choose several words and repeat them frequently. For example, if you recently got a new puppy, think of ways to say "puppy" at least five to ten times in a matter of 1-2 minutes. Write down some of the things you could say about a puppy. Remember to use the word "puppy" at least five times, i.e., "See the puppy? That puppy is little. Puppy says, 'woof woof.'" Write down what you could say about a car using *car* five times.

_____

_____

_____

_____

_____

_____

    This exercise may seem silly, but with children showing speech and language delay and also normally developing children, you may want to do exactly that during your daily routines – specifically choose certain words and use them multiple times during your interaction with your child. Frequent repetition and focus on specific words were studied by Girolametto, Pearce, and Weitzman and presented in the *Journal of Speech and Hearing Research*, Dec. 1996, in an article entitled, "Interactive Focused Stimulation for Toddlers with Expressive Vocabulary Delays." The results were very positive in terms of developing stronger vocabularies in children.

    When my youngest child was about three years old, I remember him having a very hard time learning pronouns like "he" and "she." He frequently replaced them with "him" and "her." I also remember making a conscious decision one day to focus my language on those pronouns while I played with him using his toy farm set. I produced sentences like, "He is walking to his tractor. Yes he is. He loves his tractor. He is getting in. Will he go for a ride? I think he will." Within a couple of days, my son had his pronouns straight. Focused language stimulation is an excellent tool to use, and I know it works. But I had to think about doing it – even for a speech-language pathologist, I didn't always analyze what I said to my own children.

Talk about actions.

Fill your child's vocabulary with action words that describe what he is doing and what he sees others are doing. Talking about action words also goes hand in hand with developing imaginative play, a crucial developmental skill. For example, when playing with a stuffed animal like a puppy, make it jump, run, eat, hide, and sleep. Say the words as you act them out with the puppy. You can also vary the tenses of the action words you say. Here are some examples for one action word: "Let's jump! Puppy is jumping. Do you like to jump? Let's all jump together. We jumped! We'll jump again later."

Talk about descriptions of words.

There are so many ways you can describe objects, including size, shape, color, and location. To describe a car, you could use words such as big, little, enormous, noisy, loud, quiet, long, short, or pretty. You could also describe its color and its location (in the garage). Be creative in the words you use to describe it. If you choose a descriptive word, remember to use that word at least five to ten times within a matter of a few minutes.

What if my child isn't paying any attention to me when I talk?

There will be times when you will feel like your child is not listening at all. That's fairly typical. Keep talking anyway because you may never know when your child is truly listening but just can't show it. If you notice, though, that your child is in a different world most of the time, then concentrate on being more enticing with your gestures and words. Also focus on any activity that your child loves doing with you so you can keep him engaged. Being engaged with you is crucial, and during those times your child will comprehend the words you say more easily. With children who are not attentive to others, words can sometimes be over whelming. Get into your child's interests and watch what he is doing. Copy him and see if he notices. Use only a few words in this situation to see if he reacts.

Remember to slow down.

Even though you want to put lots of information in your child's brain, don't go to the races with your speaking rate. Slow it down to help your child absorb all of the words you are saying.

How complicated should I get with my words?

There are two ways to answer this question. One possible solution is to produce words or phrases that are within a child's ability to imitate so that your child starts to produce some of those words. The other approach is to provide your child with a rich vocabulary, more complex than what your child can say. By doing the latter, you are increasing your child's comprehension skills even though your child's ability to say the words has not kept up. The answer is balance. Give both simple words and verbal models that your child can imitate, and also give words and phrases that are above your child's ability to produce. Your child needs both. Here is an example. If your goal is to get your child to imitate what you are saying, then keep your words and phrases short. When you are loading the dishwasher you could say "cup in" or "wash the cup" with an enticing voice and exaggerated movement. On the other hand, if your goal is to provide your child with rich language, in this same situation you could say, "I'm putting your blue cup in the dishwasher," or "I'm washing the sippy cup with warm water."

Choose a daily routine where you will consciously think about all of the words you can teach your child. Think about object names, action words, and descriptions. Write down some of the words you can say during that activity.

_____

_____

_____

_____

Now let's think about combining all of the techniques you have learned so far. As you **comment** about your child's world and experiences, don't forget to **wait, watch, and wonder** as he makes attempts at communicating. Give your child time to respond to the words you say. Also think about how you might **position yourself and exaggerate your words and gestures** to encourage imitation. You have completed three techniques. Let's move on to Technique Number 4.

Chapter 4

Add singing throughout your day. Children love and learn from music.

Music is a universal language. Have you ever seen children dance and sing to their favorite tune? There is no doubt about the power of music when you witness little children losing themselves in the emotion of a song.

The reason for using music to help young children learn is very simple. Children with speech and language delays need something very fundamental. They need PRACTICE. They need repetition and rehearsal daily. Because most children are attentive to music, they are more likely to sing or listen to their favorite songs over and over again. Music is one of the best tools we know to create the practice that kids need.

Adults are no different than children. Have you ever heard a song that you absolutely LOVE, and that you keep singing over and over in your head? Have you ever been moved to tears when listening to a song? Do you find yourself moving to music that has a contagious, foot-stomping beat?

Just imagine if you could make speech and language practice that contagious and stimulating. Try music.

All children, regardless of ability, can benefit from music and this technique.

Have you tried singing songs to your child? List some of them.

_____

_____

_____

_____

What types of responses do you get from your child when you sing to her? What songs are her favorites?

_____

_____

_____

_____

Write down some of the things that you feel your child may be learning from singing those songs.

_____

_____

_____

_____

If you wrote things such as learning new words, learning the alphabet, having fun with others, or doing actions, you are absolutely right. There are many other benefits to using music to enhance your child's communication, including improving imitation of words and gestures, increasing eye contact, increasing interaction with adults and peers, and following directions. When singing with your child, think about what your child is learning and how you can further expand on a song's learning potential.

The songs you choose to sing may depend on your child's interests as well as what speech and language skills your child needs to practice. The important thing to know is that whatever songs you sing, you are directly helping your child learn. If you would like some new song ideas, please go to our website, _www.TalkItRockIt.com_. Go to the FREE Resources page, where you will find lyrics to songs, or go to the _STORE_ page to see if some of our songs fit your child's needs.

In this fourth technique, we will refer to Talk It Rock It songs frequently and will also give you lyrics to some of our recorded favorites. We are not attempting to convince anyone that our songs are the best. We simply need to explain our techniques with the tools we know best – our songs. If our songs are helpful to you, we are thrilled, but remember that there are other wonderful songs on the market, and many of the best songs are those that are created by YOU – the parents and teachers of children. Here are some new ways to think about music in your child's life.

Try songs that encourage your child to interact with you.

Songs that emphasize gross motor movements are especially good for increasing your child's attention and interaction with you. One possible song to try is "Row, Row, Row Your Boat." Do it by sitting on the floor, facing each other while holding hands. On the last line, fall sideways into the "water" and brush off your bodies while saying phrases like, "My hair is wet," "my arms are wet," and "my legs are wet." After each verse, wait and watch your child. If she smiles, you know she wants more. If she gives you her hands, that's an even more obvious cue that she wants to do it again. Sing it again and again. Repetition is crucial to learning, and mutual enjoyment with a song can be used to build higher level communication skills. To continue the song, occasionally request that she attempt to say the word. If she can't, then ask her to "give you 5" to start the song again. Request something from your child, but make sure it is at the level where she can be successful. If this is a song you do not know, it is recorded in our **CD SET 1**. You may know the original "Row, Row, Row Your Boat" lyrics, which are perfectly fine to sing as well, but the Talk It Rock It version of this song, which is printed below, may be a little easier for children to sing:

Row Your Boat
Row, row, row your boat
Fishie swim.
Row, row, row your boat
We fall in.

Songs can also be used to increase your child's gross motor and fine motor imitation skills.

Any song that creates gross motor imitation is great to try. Fine motor movements in finger plays are also excellent. Children are not always able to sing the words to songs, especially while doing the finger movements, but imitation is hugely important regardless of whether it is gross motor, fine motor, or speech imitation. The ultimate goal would be to have your child do the motions of the songs AND sing at the same time. To do this, however, you will probably need to simplify something. You may want to make the lyrics simpler by changing them to vowel sounds or consonant-vowel combinations (singing "nanana" like a rock star is perfectly OK), or it may be the motor tasks you simplify by slapping your hands on your legs. One possible song or rap you could try is "Shake and Wave" from our **CD SET 3**. I have printed the words below. This song is actually a rhythmic rap that is not sung but spoken. Give your child a scarf as you do this rap together.

Shake and Wave
Shake, shake, shake your scarf. Shake, shake, shake your scarf.
Shake it in the sky. High, high, high, high, really high!
Shake it down low. Low, low, low, low, really low!
Shake it to the side. Side, side, side, side, side, side.
Shake it on the other side. Side, side STOP!
(Recite the second verse with "Wave your scarf.")

Other excellent songs for motor imitation are "Monkeys on the Bed" from our **CD Set 5** and our "Monkey Song" from **CD SET 1**.

Speech imitation can be encouraged through songs.

When selecting songs to improve your child's ability to imitate words and phrases, there is one motto to remember: Sing a simple song that I can simply sing. Your child may do well singing songs with just vowel sounds or consonant-vowel structures such as "nanana" or "bababa" as mentioned before. Any tune will do. Just let loose and let the "bababa" and "nanana" fly. Show your child that you like to sing. Your child may also be able to sing songs with single words or words that frequently repeat in chains of 3. Many of our Talk It Rock It songs incorporate simple phrases and chains of 3. For example, "Puppy, puppy, puppy. Puppy won't you play with me?" is a song that encourages imitation of the two-syllable word, "puppy."

There are other children who can sing simple phrases and 2-3-syllable words. There are literally thousands of songs that can be used to encourage that. Certainly Talk It Rock It songs stress speech imitation, but there are many other artists as well including Raffi, the Wiggles, Steve and Greg, Laurie Berkner, and Gen Jereb who have wonderful songs that emphasize a variety of developmental goals. The important thing is that recorded songs will never take the place of singing with your child. Our songs and others' are just tools to get you started, but they are meant to help parents and children engage with each other. Here is an example of a rap that encourages imitation of vowel combinations. This rap is not sung but only spoken to a rhythmic beat.

Ride the Horsie – CD SET 2
Whoa, whoa, yay, yay. Ride the horsie. Hooray!
Whoa, whoa, yay, yay. Ride the horsie. Hooray!
Ee yah (say it with me) ee yah. Ee yay (your turn) ee yay.
Ee yoe (say it with me) ee yoe. Ride the horsie. Go, go, go.

Sing the old classic children's songs.

Even if your child is unable to sing along with classic children's songs, sing them anyway. Your child is getting exposed to vocabulary when listening to these songs. Your child can also learn to imitate motor movements. Some of the most common and popular classic children's songs include: "The ABC song," "Twinkle, Twinkle Little Star," "Itsy Bitsy Spider," "Wheels on the Bus," "Five Little Monkeys," "Happy Birthday," and "Old MacDonald." When singing these classic tunes, slow down the rate of your singing, encouraging your child to sing along in any way she can. When you sing lines of a song that are repeated often, occasionally stop before singing the last word and see if your child will fill in the blank. Some children respond better to speaking raps as opposed to songs. Beloved nursery rhymes like "Humpty Dumpty" fit that category. Several of our music **CD SETS** also contain raps instead of songs for that reason.

Make up your own songs about your child's day.

You may have already done some of your own songwriting. Anytime you break into silly little melodies about your child's day, you are helping your child learn language. You can make up a song about virtually anything. When you go to the park, drive in the car, go to the store, give your child a bath, tuck your child in at night, or eat together, sing about what you are doing. You can use familiar tunes and add different words to fit the situation. The list of tunes is endless, but some of our favorites include: "Shortnin' Bread," "Skip to My Lou," "Camptown Races," "Goodnight Ladies," "Farmer in the Dell," and "For He's a Jolly Good Fellow." When you make up songs and sing them, remember that children don't care how you sing. They care that you spend time with them. Here are two examples of songs you can sing during a daily routine.

It's Time to Get Dressed (Sung to the tune, "Farmer in the Dell")

It's time to get dressed. It's time to get dressed.
Shirt, pants, socks, shoes, and all of the rest.
I put on my shirt. I put on my shirt.
I put it on my head and PULL. I put on my shirt.

(Repeat the 3rd and 4th lines of this song using the words pants, socks, and shoes for the remaining verses.)
Pants, I put them on my legs and PULL. I put on my pants.
Socks, I put them on my feet and PULL. I put on my socks.
Shoes, I put them on my feet and PULL. I put on my shoes.

I Brush My Teeth (Sung to the tune, "BINGO")
I brush my teeth in the morning. I brush my teeth at night.
I brush my teeth with a toothbrush. My teeth are clean and white.
I go ch, ch, ch, ch, ch, ch, ch, ch, ch, ch, ch.

I brush my teeth from front to back. My mommy helps me, too.
I won't be scared to brush my teeth. Because I'll be all done soon.

These are no prize-winning works, but when a child learns words for the first time because of your creation, there is no Grammy Award that can compare.

Add visuals to your songs.

When you sing a song with your child, think about how to teach your child what the words mean. Songs that contain lyrics of common objects or action words are great for illustrating or for acting out. Use pictures or the actual objects to relate to lyrics in songs. Our **CD SETS** contain visuals for all of our songs which can be printed out on a computer. We encourage you to do the same with your child's favorite songs as well. One song that you can sing and easily illustrate with pictures or actual objects is our "I Love" song, which can be sung to the tune of "Twinkle, Twinkle Little Star." If you don't have the recording from our **CD SET 2**, here is the first verse.

I Love
I love bubbles. I love rocks.
I love blankies. I love socks.
I love pickles. I love cheese.
I love orange juice freshly squeezed.
Chorus: Love, love, love I really do.
But most of all I love you.
La, la, la, la, la, la, la.
La, la, la, la, la, la, la.

Use music to help calm your child.

Music can have a calming effect on children. Soothing classical music with no words may be your best choice in helping your child settle down. Talk It Rock It has recorded some songs such as "The Owie Song" (**CD SET 1**) and "Howls and Hoots" (**CD SET 3**) to give a more relaxed and soothing beat. The song you choose to help your child calm down or transition to new situations really doesn't matter. There are some who have been successful with even playing the harmonica. You may want to sing a lullaby or hum a tune. You may be surprised what song will soothe your child.

Listen to music while driving in the car.

Children who need speech and language practice can get some of it done while riding in the car. We encourage you to sing simple songs that your child can sing, inviting her to sing along.

Talk It Rock It songs encourage children to sing along using the cue "your turn." But you should also sing your own favorites, encouraging your child to sing with you.

A word about music and its relationship to reading.

Every time you sing a song, you are preparing your child for reading. Yes, it's true. When you sing a song that rhymes, you are teaching a valuable lesson in phonemic awareness, a crucial skill that children need to be strong readers. Whenever you clap your hands to the beat of a song, you are helping your child learn about syllables in words, another crucial pre-reading skill. When you teach your child a song that emphasizes words starting with the same beginning letter sounds as in our song "Sing and Eat to the Alphabeat" – "Pizza, pickles, popcorn, too. P – P – P that's the sound that we do" – you are stressing another phonemic awareness skill. Many songs rhyme, and rhyming, too is an important precursor for reading. Not only that, songs that teach children new vocabulary will also have a direct effect on a child's later reading ability. Exposure to new vocabulary is essential for strong readers.

There are so many ways to use music that it seems a shame to give this technique only a few short pages. Our attempt is to whet your appetite about using music to help your child learn. Write some ideas of how you will try songs or raps with your child.

Let's end our musical discussion with two stories illustrating the power of music.

Two-and-a-half-year-old Michael needed to practice producing sounds that created higher tongue elevation such as "ee" and "y." He was successful at times in imitating "yeah" in therapy. His parents were very motivated to help him learn "yes" and "no," so that he could answer questions during the more frustrating times when he was not understood. When Michael's dad asked how he could help, the song "She Loves You, Yeah, Yeah, Yeah" by the Beatles seemed like the logical practice tool. Michael's dad practiced this song with Michael in the car on the way to and from daycare. The next week, guess who could say "yeah" with ease and precision? Michael could. Oh, the power of music!

William was a little two-year-old boy who had no words and had a limited ability to imitate, other than the sound, "uh." One day William's dad reported they had a new song to sing. He started the song by saying, "William, you start." So William proceeded to sing a simple song that he could simply sing. He sang, "Uh uh uh uh," and William's dad sang with gestures and a disco beat, "Staying alive. Staying alive." This wonderful rendition from the Bee Gees was powerful and incredibly touching.

Combining Techniques 1, 2, 3, and 4. As you sing songs with your child, remember the other techniques you have learned. After **singing a song**, try **waiting** and **watching** (Technique Number 1) to see how your child indicates she wants you to sing it again. Singing songs with your child and doing actions to songs achieves the goal set in Technique Number 2: Examine your position. **Exaggerate and entice with your gestures and voice**. Many songs are also filled with **commenting** about your child's world, the goal of Technique Number 3. Add a song to your daily routines and move on to the next technique.

Chapter 5

Notice when your child initiates communication. Respond and add to it.

Imagine this scenario. You come home from a very hectic day at work and tell your spouse, "I had the worst day today. Our computers shut down for over three hours, and we had tons of angry customers. One of them yelled at me for 10 minutes." Your spouse then responds by saying, "What's for dinner?" How would that make you feel if your significant other gave no acknowledgment of what you just said? I suspect it would make you feel angry or hurt. Children could feel the same way if we did not notice their communication attempts.

One of the greatest successes is when your child initiates verbally or even non-verbally to **get his needs met or his thoughts known**. These attempts to initiate might include **getting other people's attention, commenting about what he sees, requesting or asking for what he wants, greeting others, and protesting to indicate he doesn't want something.** In the hustle and bustle of our daily lives, though, it's easy to sometimes miss our children's communication attempts, especially those children who are a bit more subtle in their approach. This technique will cover two basic areas: 1) How to respond when your child initiates communication. 2) How to teach your child to initiate more frequently. Child-initiated language is your ultimate goal, so it is very important to wholeheartedly embrace the fifth technique.

Part 1 - How to respond when your child initiates communication.

When your child initiates GESTURES to communicate.

When your child doesn't initiate with words but uses gestures instead, respond by saying a word or short phrase that goes with the gesture he just did. For example, if he pulls you and wants you to stand up, say the words "Go, go, go," "Up, up, up," or "Mommy get up," as he is pulling you. If he points to a snack in the cupboard, you could say, "Do you want a cookie?" Then make a gesture of using a cookie cutter motion on your hand while you say, "Cookie, cookie, cookie please." Wait to see his reaction to what you said and watch if he attempts to imitate the gesture or words you modeled for him. If he doesn't, you could also take his hands to help him imitate the gesture or sign.

Remember that any behavior, whether it be crying, screaming, gesturing, or saying words, is communicating something. If you feel it is directed to people, those communication attempts are very powerful and can be shaped into more functional communication.

Whatever he does to initiate communication, always ask yourself these questions:

1. How can I respond to what he just gestured?
2. What can I say and do to give him new information?
3. How can I say words to make them exciting and motivating for him to try to say?

When your child initiates WORDS to communicate.

How exciting! Let's say your child just initiated the word "juice" to get something to drink. What should you do and say in response to what he just said? The biggest compliment you can give him is to imitate what he said back to him. That will affirm what he is saying as well as show him that you are interested in the content of what he is saying and not how he said it. As you imitate the word he said, you can also put that word in a simple sentence. You could say, "Oh, do you want juice?" or "You want juice!" Be sure to try to get down to your child's level and get eye contact with him as much as possible. This is especially important for children who have more difficulty achieving eye contact. They need frequent rehearsal to develop that skill of looking at people.

Next, add something to what he just said. You could add a descriptive word such as, "You like apple juice, don't you?" Perhaps try a choice question such as, "Do you want orange juice or apple juice?" Maybe use your exaggerated gestures and voice to say, "MMMMM. Yummy, yummy apple juice." At times, after saying an exciting phrase like that, wait to see if he will say it. Did you say it in such a way that it motivated him to try to say it? If he does not attempt to say the words, you could also say "Your turn," to encourage him.

The words you add are really less important than simply responding. Responding is crucial. Your great parent instincts will guide you on what to say next, and you can be confident that you will say something that helps your child learn new words to try.

Part 2 - How to teach your child to do more initiating.

As stated earlier, children initiate communication for a variety of reasons: sometimes to request something, other times to get someone to look at something, sometimes to greet others, sometimes to initiate a social game or activity, and sometimes to protest and indicate that they don't want something. Some children seem to communicate with others only to request something, and rarely use gestures or words just for the purpose of interacting with people. When thinking about teaching your child to do more initiating, it is important to think of all of the different reasons your child might be excited to communicate. If he's getting stuck on just requesting all the time, maybe you could also help him to use his words to socialize with another adult or a sibling. This section will give suggestions to teach your child to initiate communication not just to request things, but also to give and show objects to others.

There are many reasons why a child may not initiate communication with others. Some children are very passive and don't seem to have a lot of needs. They don't appear to desire the interaction with others. For those children, we need to show them that communicating with others is fun. We need to expose them to many activities and objects with the goal of finding things that are fun and that motivate them to request.

Other children have many desires but lack the skills to express those desires to others. Some children may have trouble getting their thoughts and desires out in words, so they find a way to get what they want without any help from others. Some may look like they prefer to play in isolation. The other possible reason for children lacking the ability to initiate is that some caregivers may anticipate their child's needs to the point that the child doesn't even have a chance to initiate on his own. Whatever the reason, the "Be the Messenger" technique may be helpful in teaching your child skills for initiating communication with others.

"Be the Messenger" technique – teaching your child to comment and be social with others.

To teach children to be social communicators, not only to get their needs met but to be interactive with others, there is a hierarchy of skills to teach and practice. These techniques below are cues, and my hope is to gradually eliminate the need to remind your child to participate in each of these tasks. The more you practice them, the more likely your child will be to initiate on his own.

1. **"Give it to me," or "Give it to (name of another person) please."** This teaches sharing with others and getting others to notice objects that are of interest to your child. It also teaches your child to give objects to get his needs met. Encourage this skill during snack time by asking him to share a cracker with you or someone else. You could also put small objects that he really loves in plastic containers with the lids closed tightly so he has to give you the container in order to get it open. When you are playing with

toys such as blocks with your child, occasionally ask him to "Give a block to Daddy." Being willing to include others in play by giving objects is an important step in drawing others into a child's world.

2. **"Show it to** _____**."** This skill teaches children to include others in their world by proudly showing things to people. With any toy your child enjoys, practice including other people by asking your child to show it to another person. You can also do this same technique with any artwork your child has done, any new clothes, etc. At first you would teach the command directly by saying, "Show it to __," but gradually you want to teach a child to do this skill by giving more subtle commands. Try reminders like, "I bet Daddy would like to see your picture," or "Who do you want to show your picture to?" This whole skill of "showing" things to people is the classic "show and tell" that children experience when they go to preschool programs. It's good to practice this skill at home, too. It is also important to notice if your child is looking at the person as well as the object that he is showing. That ability to shift a child's eye gaze from an object to a person cannot ever be forgotten.

3. **"Tell** ___**."** This helps a child learn to initiate communication with other people in many different ways, including commenting about what they see, sharing about what they are doing, telling people what they need, and even greeting others. Use this technique during play time and during many other daily activities. When playing with something like cars, give your child a direction such as, "Tell dad it's a car." If he is able to understand that command, gradually decrease the level of cuing by saying, "Tell dad what that is." You can also implement greetings with this technique by saying, "Tell Dad 'Bye.'" Gradually decrease that cuing as well by asking, "Dad is leaving. What do you

say?" If your child is working on short phrases, you could cue your child to call Dad to dinner by saying, "Tell Dad, 'Time to eat!'" With this technique, you give your child as much information as he needs to be successful in communicating. At first, you wouldn't be able to say a more open-ended sentence like, "Tell Dad what we did today." You may have to be more specific, such as, "Tell Dad we went to the store today," or "Tell Dad where we went today. Tell him, 'Toy store, Daddy.'"

4. **"Ask _____."** This skill helps children learn to ask others what they would like. For example, during snack time, you could cue your child to ask others a variety of questions such as, "Ask John if he wants a cookie," "Ask John if he likes puppies," or "Ask John if he wants to play." Depending on how much your child talks and how long his sentences are, you have to adjust what you expect in terms of the length of sentences your child uses. For example, if your child is eating a snack and will be sharing with others, depending on his verbal skills you could say, "Ask John if he wants a cracker," "Ask John, 'Do you want a cracker?'" or "Ask John, 'Cracker, John?'"

These four skills are all cues to teach children different ways to interact with others. Eventually, you want to decrease the cuing required to get children to initiate on their own. The amount of cuing and support is what you need to think about. How we set up the environment and structure a task depends on how your child is currently communicating and how much we need to intervene to have him be socially successful.

Here are some other suggestions for practicing the art of initiating.

Teaching commenting and increasing verbal creativity while playing with your child and his favorite toys.

When children do not initiate language with others, very often those same children are quiet while playing with their toys. They also may show decreased imagination with their toys. During a recent therapy session with one of my students, we were playing with his favorite toys: cars. Very typically, he is quiet when playing with them, and tends to put them in a line. This time I decided to start talking about other options such as going to the store and to the swimming pool in our cars. We parked our cars in the pretend parking lots, and I began to talk to my little friend about the things we could buy in the store. I gave him choice questions such as, "Should we buy milk or juice?" when he was unable to come up with any things to buy. I also asked him to tell his mom that we were going to the store and tell her that we were buying some juice. I asked him to show his favorite car to his mother. I encouraged him to ask his mom if she wanted a car. I talked to his mom about practicing different imaginative play options throughout the week with the hopes of increasing the amount of talking he would do while playing. Two weeks later, the difference in this little boy's language was amazing. He was talking about his cars, discussing where he was going in his cars, and what he was going to do when he parked his car. The more options you give a child to think about, the more he has to say.

Teaching your child to greet and compliment.

Teach your child to greet others, to give compliments, to say "thank you," and to say "please." The same need for cuing depends on where your child is currently functioning in these skill areas. Let's use the example of waving and saying, "Bye."

If your child is not yet waving or saying, "Bye," you can start by giving the direction, "Say 'Bye bye,'" taking his hand, and teaching him how to wave. If he can wave to people, but doesn't do it without being told to do so, start by decreasing the amount of cuing by just asking the question, "John is going bye bye. What do you tell him?" See if your child can then respond without being told exactly what to do. Or you may hold your hand up as a visual cue to start waving. You can also set up a role-playing situation by playing "Hi and Bye" behind a door in your house. Put a stuffed animal or another person on the other side of the door and knock. Open the door and practice saying "Hi" and then "Bye." Practice it multiple times.

Cues.

Use as few cues as possible to help your child be successful with initiating. I encourage parents to be clueless and wait a bit for your child to initiate, but never so much that your child gets too frustrated or walks away disinterested. If you sense what your child wants, see if he can convey it independently. If he cannot, you may want to ask a question such as, "What do you want?" or "What do you say?" If he cannot answer the question, you may want to try another level of cuing by holding up two objects and giving a choice by saying, "Do you want ____ or ____?" If he still is not able to respond, hold the object you think he wants within his reach. If he reaches for it, that may be the time to reach for his hand, put the object in his hand, put his hand up to your face, and then say the word in an enticing way. The level of cuing necessary is all related to how your child is currently communicating.

How does your child initiate language?

Let's analyze how your child initiates communication with others. In what ways does your child usually communicate? Does he request certain objects, show you objects, comment, greet, or protest? Give examples for each.

_____

_____

_____

_____

Now think about what types of situations you could practice with your child to improve his desire to initiate communication with others. Think of every social situation, from mealtime to playtime. Think about how you can teach your child a more sophisticated way of getting his needs met and for giving, showing, telling, and asking about his world.

_____

_____

_____

_____

Building on Techniques 1 through 5. Of all of the techniques, perhaps noticing your child's initiated language may be the most important no matter how small his attempts are. When you see these attempts, give eye contact, a smile, a verbal acknowledgment, and then add to what he said by attaching another word or phrase to it. Children who begin to initiate communication with others are truly understanding the power of it all. Let's move on to Technique Number 6.

Chapter 6

Take turns talking, giving your child time to respond. Keep it going.

Have you ever been in a conversation with another adult where you couldn't get a word in edgewise – where the person controlled a majority of the speaking time? It's frustrating, isn't it? The truth about communication is this: conversations are not real conversations unless they are a two-way street with as close to a 50/50 split in talking as possible.

When talking to your child, you want her to listen and watch you, but when you want to promote conversation and interaction with her, listening is only half of the equation. Your child needs to take her turn in the conversation. I often wonder how children feel when we don't give them equal talking time, especially children who have a speech and language delay and who cannot get their words out quickly enough to keep up with the pace of conversations around them. I would guess it feels like those times when we experience a conversation that is monopolized by another adult.

Taking turns is somewhat tricky in children who are non-verbal or who do not seem interested in engaging in the back-and-forth aspect of conversation. Can all children have a conversation? Oh yes! But we may need to re-think what a conversation really is and start with back-and-forth activities that may not involve words at all. All children, from the minute they are born, benefit from this very important Technique Number 6:

Important concept – think of "taking turns" as a conversation. This technique does not refer to a situation such as teaching your child to wait for her turn to get a balloon at a carnival. Instead, it refers to the "give and take" of activities or words that go back and forth between people. Taking turns IS conversation – plain and simple.

Taking turns with infants.

The perfect time to observe turn-taking at its best is when we hold babies. We look at the little one and say something like, "You are the cutest thing in the whole world." The baby then takes her turn by yawning, stretching, or squirming. We interpret that as a communicative turn and respond by saying, "I agree. That food made me tired, too." Then the baby starts to whimper. We respond by putting her on our shoulder and saying, "You must be uncomfortable." Oh, the joys of conversing with an infant. And we are so good at it.

When your child does or says something and you repeat it, that is considered one turn.

Keep the turns going. Some children are disinterested after one turn. That is a pretty short conversation when you look at it that way. Do whatever you can to increase the number of turns a child will take with you.

How do we take turns with a child who does not have any words yet?

There are several things to think about: 1) Be very observant of the turns your child is taking. Her turns may be subtle, as we have discussed in previous articles. 2) When you take your turn, do what you need to do to make sure she watches you. 3) Use the "wait" technique and give her a look of anticipation to show that you can't wait to see or hear what she will do when it is her turn. 4) During your child's turn, do not talk. We often have the tendency to fill in the verbal part of a child's turn. It is important to allow your child to have full control of her turn; accept all turns she takes, including non-verbal using gestures, sounds, word approximations, and real words.

You may need to make your turn so exciting that your child can't stand not to participate. Other times you may need to help your child by guiding her hand to do the activity you are doing. With turns, your child may imitate exactly what you do and sometimes she will do her own version of the turn. Either is totally acceptable.

I like to start with two basic types of activities to promote turn-taking: 1) Take turns with a bucket of toys like blocks or egg shakers, taking them out of the box one by one, putting them back in, or putting them down a tube. 2) Take turns doing a silly activity with or without an object that makes your child laugh. Sneezing objects off my head is a favorite silly activity of mine. 3) Try a game where an object goes back and forth (rolling a ball).The activity itself is really unimportant. Just use any activity where you are both able to take turns and watch each other.

When a child is playing with toys like blocks or a shape sorter, very often our tendency is to let her do the entire activity because it gives her practice putting all of the objects in by herself. Although this is certainly an acceptable way of having your child play with a toy, you will not be promoting the turn-taking that your child may need to learn for better communication. There are some children who find allowing another person a turn extremely hard to do. Those children especially need practice with this skill. With some children, you may need to have all of the blocks hidden or placed in a bag that you hold in your lap, taking only one out at a time. Too many distractions (too many objects out at a time) can interfere with children watching your turn.

Choose an activity like block-stacking and take turns. Was your child willing to let you participate? What did you have to do to be sure that she watched your turn?

_____

_____

_____

_____

_____

_____

What should I do when my child gets disinterested right away?

Perhaps your game needs to change, or perhaps you waited too long for your child to take a turn. Try a puppet (You could put a sock on your hand and pretend it is a puppet.) and pretend the puppet bites your finger. Exaggerate your reaction and then wait to see what your child does. Bath time may be a good time to explore turn-taking. With a cup, pour the water out slowly, making a "shhhhh" sound as it pours out. Give your child the cup and say, "Your turn." It is difficult to give specific activities to try because every child is so different, and each family has such different objects in their house. The key to effective turn-taking is to find activities that are fun for your child. Some children initially find any new activity scary or uncomfortable. If you sense your child has that kind of trouble with novel activities, keep persisting with them to get your child more comfortable, ultimately enjoying them. Keep exploring that, and you will find success.

How do I get turn-taking that is verbal and verbal conversation going?

You need to consider how your child currently verbalizes. At first, always combine your words and sounds with gestures. That combination seems to entice children to imitate the sounds or words. Then you may get to the point where you simply name objects while playing, while participating in a daily routine, or when reading a book. After you name the objects, you may want to use the phrase, "Your turn," to encourage your child to participate.

As children become more verbal, taking turns comes closer to an actual conversation where you balance three techniques from WE CAN TALK: commenting, asking questions, and waiting for your child to respond. Waiting is sometimes the hardest. We may not wait long enough. Very verbal siblings often have difficulty waiting for their sibling's turn. They are simply too excited or too "helpful" to wait for their brother or sister to say something.

Some additional helpful tips and reminders.

When a child takes a turn, that's great, but equally as wonderful is when your child watches you during your turn. When your child takes a turn, be sure that you don't fill in the verbal parts to her turn. Her turn is her own, so your job is to simply watch her turn quietly, followed by your verbal turn.

I have found that tubes such as toilet paper rolls are often great tools to get children to take verbal turns. Also, bucket-type containers are excellent because they create an echo when children verbalize in them. I often use only one bucket or one tube and share it, so that during my turn, the child watches me.

Building on Techniques 1 through 6. Remember now to combine all the strategies you have learned as you play turn-taking games. You have now learned to **Wait, Watch, Wonder, Examine your Position, Exaggerate and Entice, Comment, Add Singing, Notice, and Take Turns**. Always think about balance with all of these techniques as we explore Technique Number 7.

Chapter 7

Ask questions to decrease your child's frustration, but use them carefully.

I enjoy sitting in airports. I know that's a bit crazy, but I love people-watching, and airports are full of interesting people. Where I choose to sit is always a very conscious decision. I look around for a family of young children. Why? Because I love listening to kids and parents talking together.

Recently, a little boy and his mom were waiting for their flight, and he was thrilled with watching the planes come and go. The conversation went something like this: "Big airplane, mommy." Mom responded, "Yes, that's a big airplane. Do you like that airplane?" "Yeah, see mommy. More airplanes!" "Oh, you're right. There are lots and lots of airplanes. How many airplanes do you see? Should we count them?" "Yeah." "Count with me. 1,2,3,4,5 airplanes, and one over there, too. That makes six airplanes," said Mom. "Look mommy. Going up." "Yes, it is. That airplane is flying in the sky. What are we going to do pretty soon, honey?" "Go up that airplane, mommy." "Which airplane do you want to fly in?" "That airplane. I go up and up and up in the sky." "Yes, you will go up high in the sky."

I love to hear conversations like that. And this mom was a master at both Technique Number 3 and this Technique Number 7.

There are many reasons why we ask children questions:

1. We use them to clarify things that they want. "Do you want juice to drink?"

2. We ask a question to give information to a child. "Oh, are you drinking your juice?"

3. We ask questions because we are genuinely interested in what our child knows or thinks about something.

Using questions to clarify things your child wants.

Questions can be an incredible way of finding out what your child needs. One type of question to work on first is a **visual choice**. Show your child two choices of things such as snacks and ask your child, "Which one do you want?" Work on having him select one and not both of them. After he selects one, you have the opportunity to comment about what he chose, saying something like, "You want crackers. Num, num, num."

The next type of choice question is a **verbal choice.** Ask your child questions such as, "Do you want cookies or cheese?" This type of question is an easy way to get children to start saying words of their own choosing as opposed to asking them to say a specific word using a command like, "Tell me cookies." Some children are more willing to say words when you give them a choice. Saying the object last that you think he wants is often easier than the reverse order. For example, if you ask the question, "Do you want cookies or cheese?" and your child does not respond, you may have a feeling that this question is too difficult for him to understand and answer. Instead, you might want to simplify the question by slowly and clearly asking, "Cookies or cheese?" As you ask, "Cookies or cheese?" hold up both objects on either side of your face, first saying, "Cookies" (hold the cookies closer to him), then pausing before saying, "or cheese?" (and hold the cheese closer to him). Wait to see if he responds to your question with a choice.

A simple "**where**" question is also a good way to clarify what your child wants or to evaluate what your child knows. Asking "Where are your shoes?" or "Where is the ball?" is an excellent way to check whether your child understands the process of pointing and searching for things.

Yes/No questions can also be a wonderful way to determine what children want. If a child can respond with a "yes," a "no," or head nods to questions such as, "Do you want some juice?" then you can follow that by asking him to say the word "juice." If your child is not willing to attempt to say the word, you can still request him to do something to get the juice. Try saying the word "juice" while you gesture, "give me

5," and ask your child to do it. You can physically help your child to "give you 5" if he is having difficulty doing it on his own. By asking your child to do something in addition to answering yes or no, you are teaching him that he needs to use words or gestures to tell people what he wants. A good name for this strategy is the **If/then technique** – "**If** you want _____, **then** tell me _____."

Other yes/no questions can be used to teach your child simple jokes. For example, you can show your child a common object like a shoe, and ask, "Is this a ball?" Your child can answer and say, "No, it's a shoe." Giving objects the wrong name is one way to tell a simple joke. Understanding jokes is an important skill for children to learn, especially those with speech and/or language delay, because it teaches them the many different ways we can use words to interact with people. It teaches that people use language not only to get what they want but to have fun with others as well. Joke-telling also helps children understand language that is more abstract and complex.

We ask a question to give information to a child.

Giving children information about their world can be done through either commenting or questioning. For example, you can say, "I see an airplane in the sky." Or you could ask, "Do you see that airplane in the sky?" Either way is totally fine as it gives children information and draws attention to something in their world. We ask questions because we are genuinely interested.

Children love to talk about things they are interested in. If we ask them questions about what they are doing, seeing, and enjoying, it empowers them to practice saying words and phrases. There are many types of questions and some are more open-ended than others. That means that some questions have a tendency to be answered in short, one-word answers while others are asked in such a way that the child is encouraged to think about the answer and then elaborate.

"**What's that**?" is a great question to teach your child to answer, especially when he is just learning names of objects. This question is one of those, however, that tends to limit your child's productions to one-word answers. That is not a bad thing at all, but if over-used, your child will not expand to more complex questions. Once your child has learned to answer "What's that?" questions, you can quickly move on to asking other types of "What?" and "Where?" questions.

Another type of question is, "**What+doing?**" (Examples are, "What are you doing? What should I do? What is he doing? What are they doing?") This is a question that may create more than a one-word response as well as "**Where+going?**" (Examples are, "Where are you going? Where should I go? Where does this go?" and "Where is he going?") As your child progresses in language ability, you will continue to challenge him with more complex questions such as, "**What do you think will happen next?**" "**What should we do before we cross the street?**" and "**How many do you have?**" These open-ended questions give children a bigger challenge of understanding the question and formulating an answer.

The number and types of questions are absolutely endless, so it would be difficult to list them all here. What is important to know is this: questions are great to ask your children. Just be aware of what types of questions your child can answer. Your goal is for your child to be successful in answering, so we will need to simplify according to what he can do. Questions are for the purpose of keeping conversations going with your child.

Following directions – another important skill.

Questions go hand in hand with following directions. Children need to be able to comprehend both in order to be effective communicators. Commands such as "Show me the ___," "Give me the ___," or "Point to the ___," are basically the same as a "Where's the ___?" question. Occasionally giving your child these kinds of directions will help you know how many words your child understands.

Also encourage your child to follow directions commonly used in his daily routines. Have your child "be a helper" by throwing things away when you request that or by getting things that you need. Giving your child specific and predictable jobs during his everyday routines will help him comprehend the words. Be consistent with the steps and use simple language to describe what he can do within that routine. For example, can you give him little jobs during diaper changing time or bath time? Can he participate with you while you are doing laundry or taking out the garbage? What better way to learn and understand the words to his day! Learn by doing!

You can also encourage your child by helping him understand directions related to playing with toys. Imaginative play is a skill that develops hand-in-hand with language. Help your child understand directions with stuffed animals, little character toys, or baby dolls, such as, "Make your puppy jump," "Make your puppy sleep," "Make your baby eat," or "Make your baby walk." If your child does not respond, show him, and continue to give those directions as you play with him.

Choose one play activity and one daily routine with your child. Concentrate on asking him questions and giving directions. What does he understand and answer? Were there any questions or directions that your child did not understand or answer? What were they?

Now, wonder about how you can help him understand those questions and directions a bit better. What will you try? Can you try pictures to illustrate each step? Can you "show" him how to do it first? Can you make the activity exciting with your gestures and words so that you entice him to participate?

Warning! Don't forget about balance.

Asking too many questions and giving too many directions can create shut-down in children. Children do not like to be badgered any more than adults do. It is important to blend **commenting** with **questioning**, so a child does not feel overwhelmed with too many questions. For example, while reading books to your child, concentrate more on making comments about the pictures as opposed to constantly asking, "What's that?" The question, "What's that?" typically results in a one word answer. Many times, the child cannot even answer that question, so asking it only serves to reinforce to the child that he doesn't know how to participate with book reading. Stay with exciting comments and wait for your child to take a turn as opposed to bombarding him with questions. Remember, questions should be used to decrease frustration more than anything, especially when a child is first learning how to communicate. So, although questions are an important skill for your child to understand and answer, concentrate on a balance of 80% comments and 20% questions/directions when talking with your child.

As we near the end of our 9 techniques, continue to think about all of the other techniques. Balance is the key. And now, on to Technique Number 8.

Chapter 8

Laugh a lot! Laughing together is a great way to get talking started.

You can never MAKE a child talk. If a child is not saying words or is not trying to copy your words, you cannot force her to do so. There is one tool, however, that you can try that will encourage and entice your child to make sounds. That tool is laughter. Try to have so much fun that her laughter turns into verbalizing. In essence, you will be tricking her into making sounds.

Yes, laughter can encourage verbalizing, and there are also other benefits to using laughter. Laughter and humor can be used to connect children to each other, especially those who have a difficult time interacting and conversing with peers. People are more likely to laugh when they're with other people as opposed to being alone. There's nothing more contagious than laughter.

Laughter creates a social connection between individuals. Laughter is what separates humans from all of the other creatures in the world. Laughing, Technique Number 8, will be your barometer reading as to how successful you are in having a good time with your child.

This chapter will list some specific suggestions about laughter, but first I need to give some thoughts on laughter. This technique is near and dear to my heart, not only for the benefit of children and their development, but also for the benefit of the parents who care for them. Laughter has been essential to my well-being, and I feel the need to share this story.

Laughter and the benefits for parents as well as children.

Parents, I know that your children are your life. I know that when your child struggles, your heart hurts. But if you are under any stress at all, I encourage you to remember the gift of laughter. Laughter has a medical benefit that has been confirmed through research. The University of Maryland

School of Medicine has found that laughter is linked to healthy functioning blood vessels and consequently fewer heart problems.

I know very well the power of laughter. Our daughter was diagnosed with leukemia when she was six years old. There were certainly more tears during those 2½ years of treatment than I care to remember. But we knew that stress could make us ill, and it was important for us to be strong for our daughter and two sons. So, during that time of stress, my husband and I committed to having fun, to filling our house with laughter whenever possible. Laughter was a huge part of our days, weeks, months, and years. We were almost thrown out of Short Stay Surgery once when Kelsey was getting chemotherapy because we were laughing too loudly while watching the movie *Dumb and Dumber*. We are proud to probably be the only family ever to be scolded for laughing too loudly at Children's Hospital. We know that some situations do not warrant laughter – there are plenty of serious times when tears and deep conversation are needed. But we also know that laughter helped our family get through the stress, and we believe that it made us physically and mentally healthier.

Remember, too, that laughter is important for the other children in your family. If life is stressful, and the focus of your attention is on one child, having enjoyable activities with your other children is of utmost importance.

How can I use laughter to help my child learn?

Now let's get to some specific suggestions on how to reach your child with laughter. Previous techniques have encouraged you to find activities that your child has fun doing. As you already know, finding things that make your child laugh also increases your child's ability to stay engaged with you. Always explore the "laughter factor" as you help your child learn to communicate.

Children can figure out pretty quickly which adults are playing with them for the sheer joy of it all and which ones are playing with them solely to get them to say something or do something. When you are playing with your child, think about just enjoying the moment, enjoying the time together. That, more than any other technique, creates the true conversation that you want.

Caution: When we talk about laughter, please know that out-of-control tickling your child is NOT recommended. A tickle game can be very enjoyable for a child and can be the catalyst for getting children more verbal. It is important, however, that the tickling is done for a short time. One or two seconds in duration is all you need. If tickling occurs longer than that, it sends a message of, "I'm in control and have more power than you," as opposed to "I enjoy being with you." A tickle game is wonderful if you wait between the short tickles and watch for your child's reaction to look at you in anticipation of another quick tickle. If she laughs and shows you that she wants to do the game again, then you know that your approach is good. The act of tickling is not the real goal. The goal is creating laughter, verbalizing, and interaction to continue the game.

Stages of laughter.

There are five types of activities that create laughter in children. They do follow a hierarchy, but what is cool about the stages of laughter is that children do not outgrow the stages as they move to the next. They just build on the skills they already have. If you are trying to get your child engaged with you, you may want to try the first item. Laughter can be caused by:

1. Movement activities

2. Sudden or unusual behavior

3. Using one object for another

4. Playing with words and misnaming

5. Verbal and visual absurdities

Movement activities.

Some of my favorites are: swinging a child in a swing, swinging a child in a blanket with one person holding one end of the blanket and the other person holding the other, chasing and catching her, flying her in the air like an airplane and landing on the couch or bed, turning her around in a swivel chair, wheelbarrow walking, and playing interaction songs and games such as "Here Comes the Mousie," which is written below. As you recite this poem, walk up your child's leg with your fingers, ending with a tickle under her chin.

Here Comes the Mousie
Here comes the mousie living in the housie.
(Walk up her leg with your fingers.)
Is he there? (Put your fingers under one arm.)
Is he there? (Put your fingers under her other arm.)
No, he's there!

(Put your fingers under your child's chin and tickle briefly.)

You probably have done many other activities that involve movement. With any movement activity, remember to occasionally stop the activity, see if your child is laughing and having fun, and wait to see how she will initiate doing it again.

Sudden or unusual behavior.

Activities that are sudden or unexpected often create laughter. Some of these ideas such as the "Ahchoo" game have been discussed in previous techniques. You never know what will get the "laughter factor" going with your child. I once put cosmetic sponges in my glasses while I was wearing them, and my student laughed hysterically for the longest time. That silly activity set the stage for her to say words. It was totally spontaneous and something that I never used again with any other child.

Here is another example. Recently I was working with a little boy who never saw the humor in sudden or unusual behavior. I showed him a picture of an apple tree and pretended to pick one of the apples and eat it. He looked at me with an unamused look. I did it again, exaggerating my movements and verbalizing even more, and out came a little smile. The third time was a charm. I did it again and said, "Your turn." He imitated the movement with a smile on his face. His mother was amazed that he was able to see the humor in that activity and participate. That understanding of humor is a higher level language task that will be used frequently in a child's life.

It is virtually impossible to give specific suggestions, though, on what will make your child laugh. That has to be left to you to figure out. Every child is so different in what excites her. When your child laughs, wait and watch to see if she initiates having you do it again. Or watch to see if she will imitate and try to do it, too.

Using one object for another.

Some children love it when we use objects for something other than what they are intended. Grab a shoe and put it to your ear as a telephone. Pick up a hairbrush and pretend to brush your teeth. Does your child see the humor in that? This technique will not work if your child does not know the normal functions of objects, but once she recognizes their purpose, she should be challenged to see the humor in silly activities like this.

Playing with words and misnaming.

In the same manner as using objects for other purposes, we can also misname objects. Children love to correct adults making errors. For example, if your child knows the names of many objects, hold up an object such as a ball and ask, "Is this a shoe?" If your child cannot yet correct you, answer the question yourself and say, "No, silly me. That's not a shoe. It's a ball."

Also, play with words such as changing beginning sounds to create rhyming words. Children enjoy hearing the differences and similarities when you create silly sentences such as, "My cat has a hat and sits on a mat. Imagine that! Silly cat."

Verbal and visual absurdities.

When children become verbal and speak in sentences, it is important to challenge them with more complex humor. Telling jokes, beginning with knock-knock jokes, can help develop higher level language. Talk about things like animals and ask questions that are absurd, such as, "Can a donkey fly an airplane?" or "Can a cow drive a car?" You can have silly conversations about the most ridiculous things. You can also look at pictures that have visually absurd things in them. For example, one of our Talk It Rock It songs from **CD SET 2**, entitled, "No Way," illustrates many absurd situations such as a cat eating a hat and a monkey driving a car.

It's not just about LAUGHTER. Positive interaction creates positive behavior.

Laughter is important, but it is perhaps even more valuable to expand on this technique by including anything positive that you say to your child. If you remember the research study by Hart and Risley mentioned in the Commenting chapter, some parents were shown to speak much less to their children. Those same parents were the ones who directed many more negative comments to their children than the others. Use the 5-to-1 rule: 5 positive comments to every 1 negative. More than anything, speaking more positively to your child will result in more positive behavior.

One final comment – JUST HAVE FUN!!! Now let's move on to the LAST TECHNIQUE!

Chapter 9

Keep books handy. Your child needs a daily dose of reading.

There are two major contributors to developing strong readers: Talking with your child and reading with your child. It's basically that simple – talk and read. Long before children can identify a letter of the alphabet or read any words themselves, they need to have been read to thousands of times. In the age of technology, reading books is often replaced with TV shows and video games. We are competing for our children's time, and TV often wins. Let's explore some of the ways you can promote literacy throughout your day, committing to decreasing the TV viewing and increasing the time spent with books and other literacy ideas. The last technique in our WE CAN TALK series encourages you to incorporate literacy throughout your child's daily activities. Commit to this crucial technique.

Where do we start?

With young children, start looking at books at a very early age. The books you choose are very often picture books with young infants and toddlers, but they can be storybooks, too. Look at the pictures, name the objects on the page, and have a conversation about things going on in the book. Pay attention to what your child is interested in. Stories that have repetitive lines are also excellent, as they allow for the child to fill in those lines or say them with you.

If your child is not yet talking, imagine how you can put gestures into your book reading. When you name pictures, point to them with excitement and exaggerated movement.

Use sound effects and silly actions in your book reading. For example, if you see a picture of an apple, name it as you point to it, pretend to pick it up and eat it. Say "yum yum" as your pretend to eat the apple. Then WAIT. (count to 5 or 10 under your breath if you have to so that you are waiting for your child to take a turn with the book.) Does your child respond? Keep persisting on giving your child time to respond to what you doing and saying with a book. You want your child to be an active participant in book reading, taking turns at times, discussing the happenings in the book. Have a dialogue about a book.

As your child gets older, you can start reading the story, but always try to have conversations about the story as well as just reading it. Read WITH your child and not just TO your child.

Ask your child questions about what he sees, what he thinks will happen next, and what he likes. Refer to your real world with things in the book. For example, in a book about eating pizza, you could say something like, "He's eating a piece of pizza. Do you remember when we had pizza? What kind do you like?" It's also great to encourage your child to be the reader of the story sometimes.

It is totally OK to divert from the story line to have conversations during storybook reading. In fact, studies show that it is preferable to have discussions about the story, to ask questions and wonder about different things happening in the story, as opposed to just reading it. Think about dialogue you can create. Teach your child to listen AND verbally participate. Listening and speaking should have a balance of turns between you and your child.

Components of developing reading skills.

Research on literacy reveals four major skills that should be emphasized very early and throughout your child's toddler and preschool years. Provide daily exposure for your children in these four areas:

1. Oral language

2. Phonemic awareness

3. Print and alphabet knowledge

4. Emergent writing

Oral language involves the daily conversations you have with your child, and has been covered thoroughly in earlier techniques. There is nothing more important to the development of literacy than all of the talking you do with your child. Reading and writing are simply extensions of listening and speaking. Your child's listening and speaking skills will directly affect what he will be able to understand and read on a page. Throughout your day, remember to talk to your child about the things he is doing, seeing, and enjoying. Remember to ask him questions about what he sees. At the end of each day, recap all of the activities that he did during his day. Use words that he may not understand, but with repetition, will grow to have in his vocabulary. Encourage him to talk to you and keep the conversations going by responding to what your child says. These are all ideas that we have covered in earlier chapters, but because oral language is a key to literacy, it cannot be emphasized enough.

Phonemic awareness encompasses many skills including rhyming, hearing and understanding similarities between beginning letter sounds, and counting syllables in words. Invest in books with rhyme, rhythm, and repetition. Have your child fill in the phrases with the rhyming word. For example, a rhyme such as "Humpty Dumpty sat on a wall.

Humpty Dumpty had a great fall," is a perfect example of a poem that can teach rhyme. Have your child sit on your lap as you do this rhyme. When you get to the word, "fall," open your legs and have your child gently fall through.

Occasionally clap or tap out the syllables of longer words so that your child can hear the parts to the words. Animal names are especially good for tapping out the syllables. Try words such as "alligator, elephant, and hippopotamus," tapping away as you say them.

Songs are excellent for teaching phonemic awareness. Anytime you clap to the beat of music, you are teaching your child about syllables and parts of words. When we developed our Talk It Rock It songs, we focused often on rhyming and putting pictures and print to our songs so that children could "read" as they sang along. Any song can be used as a literacy tool.

Go to the public library and ask the librarian for suggestions on good rhyming books. They have far more expertise than anything that could be printed in this book.

Print and alphabet knowledge teaches your child to be aware of letters and words around him. Point out the words on cereal boxes, on logos in stores, in cookbooks and recipe cards, on coupons, and on traffic signs. In your child's play area, such as a play kitchen, fill it with words and print – notepads, grocery lists, and coupons. Have menus available from take-out restaurants so your child can use them during play. Most importantly, make comments about letters and words in your child's world. Point to letters and say, "Look, that word starts with the same letter as your name," or "That word says 'boat.' B-O-A-T. It rhymes with 'coat.'" Your child needs to hear those direct comments about the print. It's not enough to place the print in his midst. Direct teaching is necessary to derive meaning from those words. Keep in mind that your child learns a lot from watching you. "Print knowledge" is learned when he sees you reading magazines, books, and catalogs for fun and as part of your work.

Emergent writing can be encouraged once a child is able to hold a writing tool like a crayon, marker, or pencil. Scribbling, painting, and drawing pictures all set the stage for teaching your child writing skills. Drawing straight lines and circles are merely beginning stages of letters and can be shaped into that. In your child's play area, have notepads available so your child can draw or "write." (Of course you run the risk of having works of art drawn on the walls, so you will have to work through that rule first. I still remember painting my friend's wall with black paint when I was about four years old.) When you are writing a grocery list, have your child write one, too. It doesn't matter that your child can't write. He just needs the opportunity to try. Match coupons to store newspaper ads. Write a letter to a grandparent. Pretend to make letters, put them in an envelope, and create a mailbox in your play area. But most important again is to point out these things to your child. When he draws a circle, for example, tell him he just made an 'o.' Tell him that by putting a line on one side, it makes a 'd' and the other side makes a 'b.' Kids need the specific teaching, but done in a playful, spontaneous way. This is emergent writing.

What should I do if my child is not into books at all?

Some of your child's daily adventures can be easily incorporated into a book. Talk about what he did during the day and write those things down. Turn it into a book by using your or your child's artwork and photographs to illustrate them. Look at photo albums with your child and write captions or story lines about each picture. If you can think of a sentence that rhymes to describe the picture, it may make your child more interested in listening to it. Pictures about what your child is doing are probably the best. You can create a "language experience book" with your child as the main character.

A nice step up from a family photo album is a children's book with real photographs. Often, these books are simple and colorful, so they may capture your child's attention. Your child may like looking at photographs of babies and kids, animals, familiar vehicles, toys, foods, and items found around the house.

Go to the library or bookstore and find books that have very simple, rhyming, and repetitive phrases in them. They will likely capture your child's attention better than other books. You could also choose books that have pockets or doors that open, pop-up books, or books that have touchy-feely items, as these create interest. There are also some books that have built-in puppets. Those have been helpful in my work with children. Keep persisting, trying out book after book, until you find one that your child is interested in. Do not ever give up on reading to your child. You will have to adapt and brainstorm, but don't give up.

Sometimes have your child sit on your lap, but other times, sit across from each other. That gives you more opportunity to use facial expressions to capture your child's interest with the book. It also promotes the skill of joint attention: being able to shift attention from an object (the book) to a person (the person reading the book). Using gestures, an animated voice, and excitement will keep your child attending longer.

With picture books of things like animals, I would become a part of that book by petting the animal, kissing it, pretending it is nibbling my finger, beeping his nose, anything to draw attention to the picture and you simultaneously. The more silly you can get, the more likely your child will stay with the story.

Lastly, choose books that have pictures of high interest to your child. If your child likes airplanes or trains, find a book about vehicles. If he likes animals, get a book about the farm or the zoo. Your child's interests are key, but at the same time, if there is a children's book that you love, your excitement will come through. Use those books, too.

If you are having a tough time getting your child to sit or show interest in book reading, keep the story time short. Focus on books that contain pop-ups, real photos, or just a VERY short book with simple pictures. Length of story reading is really the key at first to getting your child interested. Keep it short, simple, and positive.

List some of the changes that you will incorporate to promote reading with your child. From the suggestions in this chapter, what will be possible for you to start using?

Were you ever read to as a child?

If your caregivers never read to you as a young child, it is sometimes difficult to get into the habit of doing that for your child. If there would ever be anything that you could do that would have a long-lasting impact on your child's future, it would be reading. It's not just what I think. It's what I know, and it is proven time and time again in research. Read WITH your child, have conversations about the books, and relate them to your real world. Commit to daily reading, and you will reap the benefits as you see your child grow.

Congratulations! You have learned the 9 WE CAN TALK techniques for enhancing your child's speech and language skills.

Chapter 10

Summary and closing comments.

Over the years I have seen many parents playing and interacting with their children. All of them have been instinctively good at the "game" of enhancing their child's speech and language. As a speech-language pathologist, it is my job to tell you that and point out the specifics of what you do that are so great. This book is meant to be more for fine-tuning the skills you already have and for empowering you to know that what you are already doing is excellent.

Regardless of how much education I have in speech and language development, children can still stump me sometimes. It is tough to know exactly what to do when children throw you a curve ball that you haven't hit before. Sometimes I strike out, and you will, too. It's all a part of the game of teaching your children to communicate. I like the baseball analogy, because batting .300 is actually a sign of a great player. The key is that they never give up. They simply analyze what possibly went wrong, get up and try again, and LOVE every moment of the game. That's my goal when I work with children – to LOVE every moment.

These 9 techniques can be your general book of guidelines as it has been for me for many years. They have helped me analyze and problem-solve for years now and have served me well. For the parents who are reading this book, I encourage you to seek out a speech-language pathologist who can "coach" you when you are stumped by something. A book like this can never take the place of person-to-person observation and interaction. For the speech-language pathologists who are reading this book, always be available to give those practical suggestions to parents when they need them. Honing our skills in the area of speech and language enhancement during practical, daily routines is crucial to every child on our caseload.

Parenting is the toughest but most rewarding job you will ever have. Unfortunately there is no instruction manual that comes with each child. We can only learn as we go, throwing out what doesn't work and expanding on what does. There is a simple way to take these 9 skills to a basic theme: spend time talking to, listening to, and watching your child as he attempts to communicate with you. When you do this, you will know that you are doing a great job. Be confident of that!

Best wishes to you and your family.

Rachel Arntson, M.S., CCC, Speech-Language Pathologist

Products available through Talk It Rock It.

Rachel Arntson, speech-language pathologist, co-founder of Kids' Express Train, and owner of Talk It Rock It, had a desire many years ago to create products that would enhance the speech and language skills of children. Because music is such a powerful tool, Rachel began writing simple songs to help children imitate sounds, words, and phrases. As a result, Talk It Rock It now has 5 CD sets containing songs, printable illustrations, and a manual. In addition, Talk It Rock It also provides the WE CAN TALK book, the Push-Pull Puzzle, Animation Station audio-visual shows that can be viewed with a DVD, computer, or iPad, and many other products to enhance the speech and language of young children.

Every song I have used from these CDs has been a hit. They are engaging and lively and provide excellent home speech and language practice.
Carol Hanson, CCC-Speech-Language Pathologist

Seminars available through Talk It Rock It.

Rachel's seminars:
Rachel focuses on teaching others how to enhance speech and language skills in children using simple but effective techniques. She presents one-hour to two-day seminars with an emphasis on two primary themes: using music to increase speech and language skills, and helping children communicate by teaching seven basic communication skills and the 9 parent training techniques from the WE CAN TALK book. Rachel designs her seminars with the particular desires and needs of the audience. Whether you are a parent, teacher, speech-language pathologist, early intervention provider, daycare provider, or other early childhood educator, these seminars will provide you with excellent information presented in a lively and entertaining way.

Rachel's presentation was the best one of the conference! Her topic was amazing, yet any topic would have been great to hear from Rachel! The session was very practical, and I have so many ideas that I can apply to my students tomorrow! Thank you for re-energizing me for the end of the school year. I was inspired and would love to hear her again.

Feedback from a speech-language pathologist following the CESA 5 Speech-Language Pathologist Institute in Wisconsin Dells, Wisconsin

Rachel Arntson Biography:

Rachel Arntson, M.S., CCC-SLP, has been a practicing speech-language pathologist in the greater Minneapolis, Minnesota area since 1980 with a specific interest in using music to enhance the speech and language skills of children. Rachel has recorded 9 CDs (2 in Spanish), has written a parent training book entitled, WE CAN TALK, and has created other products that provide simple, engaging speech and language practice for young children.

She co-founded Kids' Express Train, LLC in 2002, and in August of 2012, began a new company entitled TALK IT ROCK IT. Rachel is excited to continue her passion of providing practical speech and language materials and songs. She continues to work full time with infants, toddlers, and their families in an early intervention program in Minneapolis. In addition, Rachel presents nationally and internationally, sharing her passion for music through creative and interactive workshops.

Most importantly, Rachel is very blessed with a wonderful family – a caring husband who supports her in the Talk It Rock It business and 3 beautiful children who have brought her tremendous joy.

Explore our Talk It Rock It website:
For further information about our products and presentations, visit our web site or contact us by phone, mail, or email.

Our address:
Talk It Rock It, LLC
P.O. 1734
Maple Grove, MN 55311

Web site: www.TalkItRockIt.com
Email: Info@TalkItRockIt.com
Toll free number and fax: 1.888.530.7773